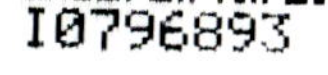
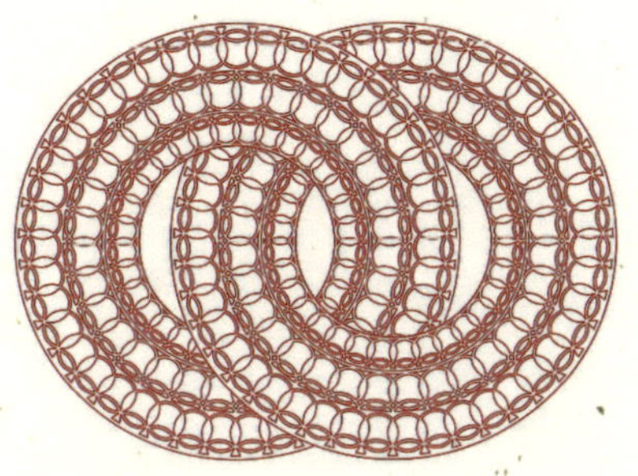

Dead Things and Where to Put Them

Dead Things *and* Where to Put Them

Marina Carreira

CavanKerry Press Ltd.
Fort Lee, New Jersey
www.cavankerrypress.org

Publisher's Cataloging-in-Publication Data
provided by Five Rainbows Cataloging Services

Names: Carreira, Marina, author. | McEniry, Lynne, writer of foreword.

Title: Dead things and where to put them / Marina Carreira ; foreword by Lynne McEniry.
Description: Fort Lee, NJ : CavanKerry Press, 2025.
Identifiers: ISBN 978-1-960327-13-0 (paperback)
Subjects: LCSH: Luso Americans--Poetry. | Queer poetry. | Grief--Poetry. | Divorce--Poetry | COVID-19 Pandemic, 2020-2023--Poetry. | American poetry--21st century. | BISAC: POETRY / LGBTQ+ | POETRY / Subjects & Themes / Death, Grief, Loss. | POETRY / American / Hispanic & Latino. | POETRY / Women Authors.
Classification: LCC PS3603.A77 D43 2025 (print) | DDC 811/.6--dc23.

Cover artwork: Genesis Bosse
Author photo: Ysabel Y González

Cover and interior text design by Mike Corrao
First Edition 2025, Printed in the United States of America

Florenz Eisman Memorial Series

CavanKerry Press is proud to present the seventh book in the Florenz Eisman Memorial Series--fine collections by New Jersey poets, notable or emerging. A gifted poet and great lover of poetry herself, Florenz was the publisher partner in establishing the press and CavanKerry Managing Editor from its inception in 2000 until her passing in 2013. Her ideas and intelligence were a great source of inspiration for writers and staff alike as were her quick wit and signature red lipstick.

Made possible by funds from the New Jersey State Council on the Arts, a partner agency of the National Endowment for the Arts.

NATIONAL ENDOWMENT for the ARTS
arts.gov

CavanKerry Press is grateful for the generous support it has received from the New Jersey State Council on the Arts, as well as the following funders:

The Academy of American Poets

Bergen County Arts

Community of Literary Magazines and Presses

National Book Foundation

New Jersey Arts and Culture Renewal Fund

New Jersey Council for the Humanities

New Jersey Cultural Trust

New Jersey Economic Development Authority

The Poetry Foundation

ALSO BY MARINA CARREIRA

I Sing to that Bird Knowing It Won't Sing Back, 2017

Save The Bathwater, 2018

Tanto Tanto, 2022

Desgraçada, 2023

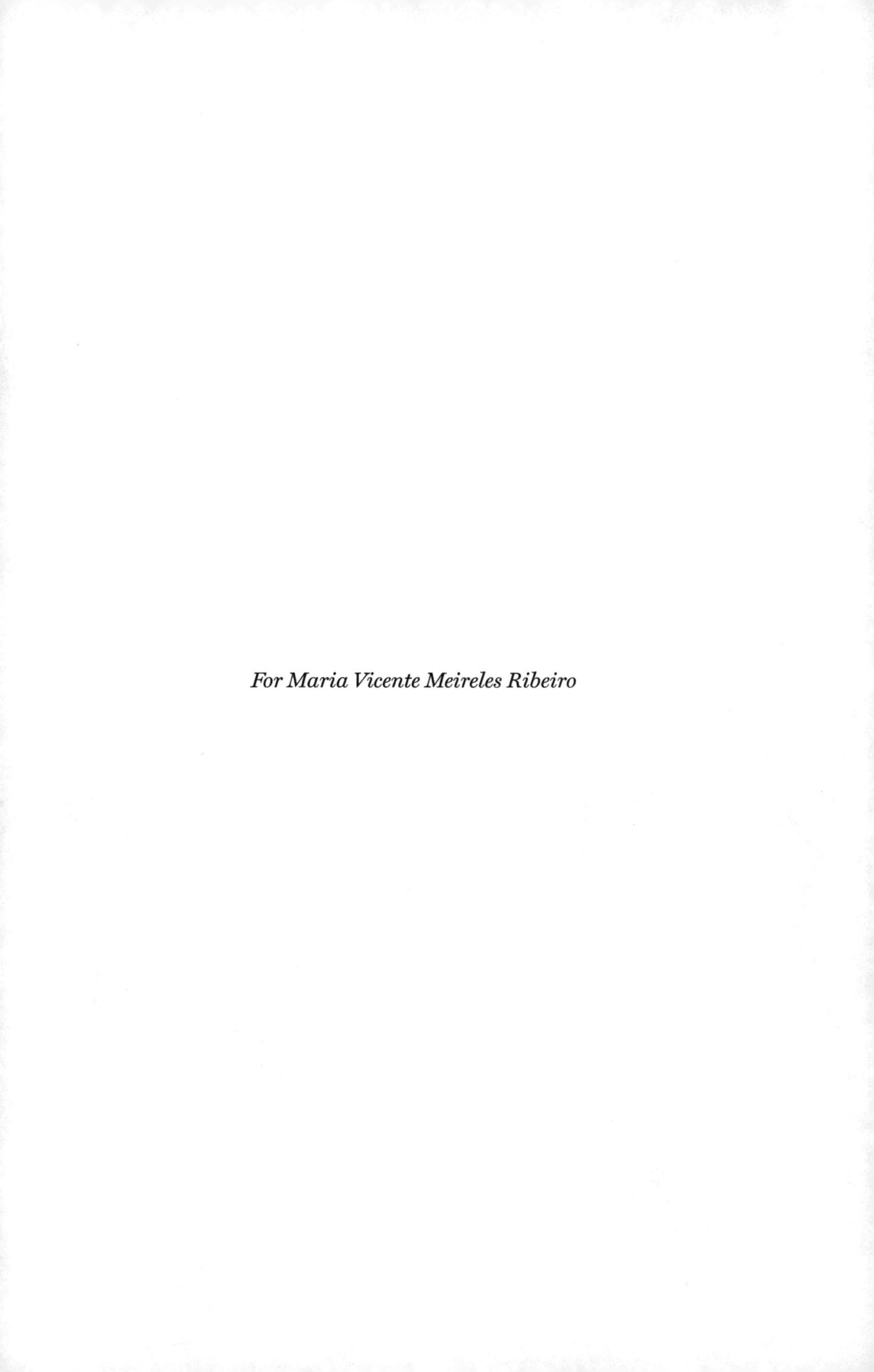

For Maria Vicente Meireles Ribeiro

I have all of these lily plants, but not you, nor peace

— Kamilah Aisha Moon

by all my loyal dead. I have learned
to crawl backward into the wilderness

— Rachel McKibbens

If they only knew how tenderly
memory's fingers caress
how expertly

— Tamara Zbrizher

CONTENTS

Foreword

In a world that often shies away from that which we cannot save, Marina Carreira embraces it all. She's learned to hold the dead—the memories, the lost, the broken—and give them a home in her heart . . . not as burdens, but as companions. *Dead Things and Where to Put Them* isn't just a collection of poems, it's a litany of resilience, tenderness, and defiance in the face of everything life throws at us; each poem a reminder that even in our deepest grief, there's a fierce joy in living fully, right now.

At the heart of this collection is the title poem—a tribute to the oceanic struggles and waves of prayer that define the lives of women who hold their families, their cultures, and their faiths close. It speaks to the profound connections between generations of women who keep alive traditions of both language and spirit. These are women who move between worlds, possibly without fully belonging to either. Yet, in their constant negotiation of space and place, they find strength and grace.

Woven through these poems is an unbroken thread of devotion—devotion to family, to faith, to identity, to poetry and the natural world, and ultimately to the joys and the chaos that stretch across generations. These poems carry the rich echoes of saints whose stories intertwine with the vibrant lives of Portuguese women, both in their ancestral land and in the immigrant neighborhoods of Newark, New Jersey. Through these women, the sacred, the personal, and the communal merge in beautiful rhythms of love and loss.

With these poems, Carreira invites us to journey through grief, memory, and transformation. The book is an atlas of loss—each poem a map guiding us through the strange, sometimes unsettling places we find when we dare to look closely at that which we often wish to bury: The dead things. The forgotten things. The things that refuse to be forgotten. What Carreira offers here is a deep reckoning with what haunts us, what hides at every turn, and with what refuses to remain hidden along the path.

I am continually in awe of how Carreira makes the invisible visible, how she takes the intangible and makes it something we can feel in our bones. Every word in this collection has weight, texture, and a rhythm that carries us, whether we want to be carried or not. It is impossible to read these poems and not be changed by them. Carreira has distilled grief and beauty, memory and future, loss and love into something that burns with a quiet, fierce light. This is not a collection of easy answers; it is a collection of questions and of invitations to understand the dead things we carry with us in a way that lets us finally begin to let them go—or at least learn where to put them.

The language of these poems pulses with the melodies of the Portuguese tongue—sometimes soft and lilting, sometimes forceful and persistent. These poems speak of generations learning to love the world one comes from and the world one now inhabits. The prayers uttered, the love given, and the memories passed down are acts of survival and of profound beauty.

Each poem in this collection is a testament to resilience and a prayer to the saints who guide the dead. The poems are a celebration of what it means to be a woman who is both rooted in and battling with religion/faith . . . a woman tied to history, forever bound by the legacy of those who came before and relying on them to support her as she navigates this world full of hate, brutality, and fear, with an urgent need to seek out the empathy and grace necessary to experience love, mercy, and joy.

Dead Things and Where to Put Them is a raw testament to Carreira's courage and the depth of her spirit and showcases her deep commitment and connection to the dead, the dying, and the trying to live. In every word, I see the authenticity of someone who is not afraid to confront the darkness, and the unflinching bravery of someone who refuses to be defined by it. Carreira makes space for harsh truths and unconventional beauty in these poems. I aspire in my own writing to master her skill for being both completely unguarded and fiercely unapologetic. These poems embody her ability to show what it means to be fully alive, even in the face of everything that threatens and *does* take that life from us.

Conjuring what she can of her grandmother's wisdom to see herself through this life, Carreira reminds us, in the fourth poem of the collection, *O Que Não Mata, Engorda*:

> *Ai ai,* you would mutter, *o fim do mundo.*
> *Ouve lá,* you would ask, *já comeste?*

May these poems, with their beauty and honesty, live forever close—at hand and heart. May they continue to echo long after you read them, and may you return to these pages as you explore and discover where to put your own dead things.

— Lynne McEniry
January, 2025

To the Mother Rabbit in My Backyard

The crow came and swooped the first
of your litter. You chased it across the yard
until the fence let you no further.

When it returned, I ran out and hollered,
arms wild, but its talons were already through
the second kit's ribs. You hopped

to the last one, its tiny neck in a pool
of burgundy. I prayed it all a bad dream,
waited for bunnies to spring up like crocuses,

mouths ready for green and air.
But the empty, trimmed grass displayed
our loss: your offspring; my naivete.

Afterward, you sat in mourning,
in the coldest rain this April, still
except for the occasional twitch.

Chaos cut through every blade
and all I did was watch
your grief from my window.

How do you tell a child
death comes quick? You don't.
You draw the shades,

serve up eggs and toast
for breakfast, tell her to chew
every bite extra slow.

Desgraçada

I was a dream before I was cargo
in Mãe's belly. A hazy sunrise
over an underwater canyon,
a pearl clutching sand
the way ocean does sound.
When I finally arrived, red and wet
from the crossing, I wailed my first
fado, deep as the well in Avô's
abandoned orchard. I was pronounced
patron saint of saudade and paucity.
My body—a suitcase they never unpacked.
A persimmon where a heart should be.

Penumbra

A squirrel paws through patches in my front yard, looking
for as much sustenance as his tiny arms can gather before
the frost. There are no signs of winter yet, but my muscles

are twine, my blood's a fluvial rush to the top of my brain
while my skin is still on a summer hike, basking under the glory
of our taken-for-granted star. It's okay to not be okay

with this new normal—remote learning, unlearning,
nursery-rhyme news spewing from screens, the burnt coffee,
toast and rice and meat like lead in our bellies,

children humming songs about bluebirds they only know
from books. It's okay to bite every curse your grandmother
taught you in half, so that one part sticks to the roof of your mouth

like a spell, the other flies off into God's ear so She knows
this team spirit will not last. "Mommy, do we have to die?" Simone asks.
I want to scream, *Stop that, you're four years old and death should be*

the last thing on your mind! I want to say, *No! We will live forever and ever*
and only dogs die. Instead, I tell her, "Yes, but it's okay," and she runs off,
singing about the sun, the moon, the magic spaces in between.

O Que Não Mata, Engorda

Raised on olive trees and
their switches, seven siblings,
Salazar, East Newark in the 70s,
you wouldn't listen to doctors say,
"Wash your hands several times a day,
expectorate into your elbow."
You'd scoff, blow your nose
with yesterday's tissue, tell them,
"Only animals sneeze on themselves."
Today an older man at the market
said, "Step back, six feet please," while
he grabbed too much bread for two.
A tired woman with a face mask sliced
the chouriço like a sad violinist.
What do you see from your sealed
hospital window besides an ocean
you don't bathe in, a sun that hasn't
cloaked your bones in weeks?
Here, I conjure you up, what I've left
of your wisdom to get me through
while my partner watches
videos on food preservation.
"This is how we survive," she says.
"We can store cheese in salt for months."
"Ai ai," you would mutter, "o fim do mundo."
"Ouve lá," you would ask, "já comeste?"

Fazer Figa

My father's mother used to do it too—
fix her fingers in a fleshy mini-cross
to ward off evil eyes and witches,
peril and pox.

To remind her
Jesus would come again
to rule over mankind, to forgive
every man with a heavy hand and
tongue.

After returning from the river
with a sagging load of clothes,
she passed one house and another,
fitting her thumb between its index and middle
siblings, a figa
after every "Boa Tarde!"

The Forest for the Trees

Instead, you took a sharp left
and walked alongside hungry crickets.
You did not get your arm pulled,
your back crushed against pine,
but ended up in the next town,
where a woman who looked like
Avó offered you café e pão quente,
while she prepared meals
for her sons who'd be up soon
to tend graves.

His hand did not
slice you in half, his breath did not
suck air out of your lungs;
you thanked Maria and headed
home, deliberate and intact.
You did not sit under the running
shower humming *Me and a Gun;*
did not paint the pillow with terrible
ache. You put on your favorite
T-shirt and turned off the lamp.
You kissed little sister goodnight,
drew a forest in the morning.

Newark Penn Station

We drop off leftovers under the bridge, hand them
to a man smoothed red by wind and wine.

It is unseasonably warm, and I'm grateful for it,
watching a group layer old comforters and torn bags

around each other. Driving away empty, I remember
Mary in Singapore: if the world were only pain and logic,

who would want it? Still, I struggle with how men
are capable of leaving each other behind.

How millions starve while millionaires stack
bricks and steel around them. And the worker bees, we buzz

on trains, tired, numb, coffee in tow, while soot-stained altars
set up to an invisible God tremble against the tracks.

Meditations on a Mid-Life Crisis

It is raining torrentially. I should be writing and not singing, but about what? I hate my job, I want a red pickup, and my grandmother is still dead. My silly brain still can't decide between giving up and knowing when it's over, and like all things, there's a meme or TikTok for these feelings looping in my feed. Looping, that's a good word, that's what I'm doing every day, circling the kitchen and the backyard phone and school and work and supermarket, every surface and space that needs my hands and my feet that know "freedom's just another word for nothing left to lose" and grief is so bright and determined like a flame but still Beyoncé tells the world it won't break her soul and I sing along trying to believe I won't fall apart in the midst of my Mid-Life Crisis and that even if I do, the pieces will land somewhere and Mary's metaphorical wild geese will come and pick them up one by one, put all of me back together again like the ragdoll Avó made from ripped cloth and rock as a child and God I wish I was a child again so I'd know what to not do with my dumb prose, my stupid heart, my one wild and precious life

Ode to the Deer on the Side of the Road as America

Your ears still twitched two minutes after the crash,
after someone who thought himself superior
sped maniacally down a one way in the dark.
How could he have known you'd be there?
He who sees himself center of the universe;
how could he know you belong to this earth too?
That this space is yours as much as his, or mine,
and really, weren't you here first? Isn't this
documented biblically, scientifically, historically?
By the time we got to you, it was too late;
despite the small pulse from your body, I knew
death had come with its heavy boots and bag.
Blood poured from your mouth, a tiny creek
trickling back to its source. Haplessly, we called
the police, as if they would be of any use.
The officer shrugged, said he'd call for your removal,
insisted you "never had a chance," given where you "wandered."
As if the fir and field behind you weren't home.
As if your freedom wasn't as precious as his.

The Music of Animals

the howl a rusting
bucket of stars
over pines so resin
becomes muscle
over Earth's face
caws like lightning
skin the evening
so every anthill's a vein
on my pinned arm
this music covers
my *please* so that
the forest is opus
of wild dog here,
great gull there,
pernicious beast
between the air thick
and juicy beginning of
August and everyone
opens wide
the doors of dreams
my lip balm melts
in my jean pocket
while the hare sings
for her dead babies
I lay like a worm
listening to wind
and whales the ocean
just five miles away
but I drown
in the sweet
whine of a small
red fox looking
for home

Cathexis

"Careful not to drown each other,"
my therapist warns. I tell her
my partner and I are both Aquarius,

that I dreamt she left me for another
life. I never considered how this love
could swallow me whole until my limbs

burst and are remade brick.
I've always thought this love
a revolution of lavender,

a warm compress on the belly
of illness, a Hollywood dingy
in the movie storm of my life.

But the tide is coming in strong
with doubt, ebb and flow revealing
rot. Memories of better days at sea

do nothing to quell the undertow.
Truth is, love's always sunk me—
renegade mermaid I watch

at a distance from
the wreckage,
more hook than fish.

Folklore

Avó taught us monsters crawled out of woods
on rainy nights. Climbed roofs, ready to fall
from blackened chimneys unless we set a pot
of boiling water to burn them alive as they
came down. I believed this until I saw them
in the open, trading woods for Wall Street,
nightclubs and the World Wide Web. None
ever ruined unless their demons crept out
from the caves of their own hearts, and
certainly never hunched over anything but
the devoured. I've walked miles and miles
and miles away from that hard earth littered
with pine needles and bottles, to a plane of
endless juniper, sea spreading itself beneath.
On this side of recovery, Snow White runs off
with the maid. Little Mermaid screams herself
back into existence. The witch feeds Hansel
and Gretel her own limbs, nary a part to waste.
In the Church of Make-Believe, a Holy Mother
recites psalms with blade in mouth,
our fists, clutched and candle-lit.
"Such crazy talk," women with wolves
for husbands say. Folklore:
that you walk out of the forest
the same way you walk in.

Ten Ways of Looking at a Mother

I. The ugliest parts of the human body are beautiful
because of a mother. Elbows, armpits, the soles of your feet.
Her balm is there like marble.

II. Atom in Adam.

III. The forest for the trees.

IV. Someone asked the other day, "how does one survive on no sleep
for almost a year?"

To which one replies, "I feel like I've been sleeping my whole life,
'til now"

V. I once watched a finch fly into a window,
her broken body drop to the ground
like a rock in a river.

That night I prayed to a Holy Mother
weary of my worries
that its life was in sacrifice to the one

I had growing inside me. Still, I wondered
why there had been no blood.
Why it never made a sound.

VI. The core in corpse.

VII. Under the moon, the night-blooming cereus
releases its perfume, petals like a slip, mouth open wide,
hungry with wonder.

VIII. A troubling of goldfish is a Monday inside a mother's mind.

IX. Murderer, if you make her.

X. King Solomon should've known all along.

The real mother could never bear half.

Flower Moon

Astrologers say this moon in Scorpio
is where we welcome the death

of an old life, an old identity, old ways
of being. I could use a new life, a new conscious.

This one feels fractured, spills memories
like guts in a balde of vinho d'alhos.

This one is a broken, sequined diary.
This life's been a one-way trek up

Misery Mountain, toes curled at the edge.
Hell, I don't even know what I mean anymore,

just that I never imagined The End
to look like this: breakfast at nine, homeschool

from 10:30 to 12:30, then lunch, remote
work and cleaning in between. By dinner,

I'm clogged dry with coffee and emails,
lists of flowers I'll plant and herbs I'll forget

to take. I blame my follies on this flower moon
and not the woman breaking my heart.

I sit in my tub and fill it with tears until
I am under everything warm and wavy,

far from the new normal. Before bed, I'm a hare
baring her teeth at the Goddess who swallowed

my dreams and left an egg in their place.
She'll mistake this for a smile, like everyone else.

Pandemic

I've been ready for the End Times
since Avó adjusted the rusty antennas,

turned up Telemundo, watched American-
formed wars and famines in Spanish,

muttered, "É o fim do mundo" to no one.
I sat by the open window and looked

out at the sanitation guys toss bags
heavy with the Old World, police dash

down East Ferry in a fury to lock up
someone just trying to survive.

When Amalia was born, my body became
pandemic; believed I would kill her

if I didn't wash my hands a billion times,
skin raw as meat, toys sanitized

till they broke, binky boiled to death.
She grew up to show me living things

get sick and live anyway. Today, I watch
neighbors swarm the ShopRite to load up

on overpriced nonperishables and bleach,
Amazon sell out of masks and Purell,

stock markets plummet, and men
in charge make terrible decision

after terrible decision, always putting
human interest last. The irony of folks

that hate the poor and migrant
trying to flee from their contained cities.

Some things never change; some people
never will but I've learned everything

but death is inevitable. When the end
of the world comes, I'll await its arrival

the way Avô greeted every morning
in his old age: peeling an orange

extra slow, delighting in how
it leaves our chins smelling.

Haibun for My Hair

Sweet mane who comes to bat for me every morning, silently endures the push, pull, and roll of blow out, scrunch, twist, and bun—how I've let you roam at will, run amuck during shelter-in-place. You, running down neck and back without care for poise, for pinning, for damn-near-perfect. Majestic locks of brown musk, you wave, bunch and flyaway like gazelles through grasslands dodging predators disguised as clips and ties, you Plath poem on her good days, you Chapman and Winehouse lovechild, you death metal hair band at best, smooth jazz quartet at worst. Caterpillar in mouth while I type, butterfly on cheek while I snore, mound of ripe pineapple, pretty pelt of crocheted dream, fleece of summer dusk, eucalyptus on fire, singer of storms—I give you this glorious freedom

for as long as this
unknowing strongholds the rest
of this fraught body.

Perfect Circles

after Laura Boss

The best teacher I ever had
said *never say never*
especially in the morning

The best lover I ever had
showed ache is a rose
by any other name

The woman I loved most
proved you don't always go
when you leave

I used to draw circles
in my notebook
just to feel perfect

It Is a Serious Thing Just to Be Alive

after Mary Oliver and Brigit Pegeen Kelly

Take the goat. Raised as playmate to a girl,
illiterate, oldest of seven. They cross field
after field, day after day, in search of
small wonders under the hot sun. Neither
the goat nor the child knows what is to come,
that the bright joy between them is not meant
to last. *It is a serious thing just to be alive,*
to hold life in your arms, stroke it and smell it
and breathe it and feel the head call to the heart,
tell it there is no sweeter thing. *The heart dies*
of this sweetness. Months later, the goat
is slaughtered for a Sunday meal. The girl sits
at the table, hands wrung, hums a song she sang
to the animal days before its demise.
A bleating, a bleeding. A jingle in the air, years after.

Pai Eats Pie

You'd never touch pizza before now,
or a burger, much less a piece of apple pie.
But since Mom's been in Portugal, you grill
all-beef burgers and chicken dogs on a Monday
night because we're over for dinner,
and if she was here it would've been a nut log
from Nasto's for dessert, but instead
we brought pie, which I cut a small slice of,
that you ate before having your coffee and port.

Is this what love becomes? A craving
for something that's old hat to someone else?
A complete shedding of guilt and guard,
onion layers grown over years of fighting
over who fucked up, who snores the loudest.
Is it the 3000 miles apart, forced by cultural
duty to dying mothers, that lets love's
purest breath sweep through our bones
and bind us to the most complete part
of ourselves, how we ultimately become
whole, again, alone?

You smile now, especially
when you look off into the distance,
reminisce about being free after Salazar's men
captured you and your comrades,
smirk when you warn us
there will never be a true uprising
until the poor truly rise up. You laugh too,
before you fall asleep on the couch,
dream that you meet yourself again—
seventeen, by the ocean, unmarried,
unmoored, a time and place before pie.

On Earth Day

I ran to Lowe's and bought geraniums for my manicured garden
red ones like the way blood spreads over skin after a cut
they remind me of the old house in Fanhais, rustic split level
in our family for three generations, two geranium pots posted
at the door, guard to pest and ghost I spill the old soil
from the rusting vase and plop the plant in, surround it
with fresh earth If Eden had flowers I bet it would be geraniums
not just red ones but all hues and shades How paradise could have
bloomed had no human been planted I wonder if the only way
we can survive this is to perish, so that Earth can evolve again,
not with people but eucalyptus and thyme, poppies and pine,
jasmine and geraniums, where hummingbirds and butterflies run
the kingdom and I am merely a rumor from an old crow's mouth
"the one who tried to keep us alive but not herself"

Prayer to Saint Philomena

A viúva told me: pray to Philomena—
that she grant your daughters immunity
from every serpent oil sold them
on Instagram. You, meek statue

on my sill, charged with shielding them
from horrors I've imagined twice over
before this pandemic began. By a faith
older than man's imagination, free them

from the sparkly vice this world uses
on girls, the one where nothing squeezes
through but prescribed gender play:
perfumed stationary, mink lashes

and red bottoms, diamond-studded
bodies, tiny waists, perfect asses.
Let this, too, pass, so that I can say,
"We didn't survive a goddamn plague

for you to turn around and think youth
is Sephora skincare and TikTok fame.
Your foremothers didn't endure apocalypse
after apocalypse for you to be so basic,

to believe you are not more than the madness
spoon-fed you by patriarchy." Philomena, child
martyr who traded virginity for salvation,
knowing nothing of either;

scourged, drowned, shot
and decapitated by men old enough
to be your father, save all women
from the myths that did you in.

May the only anchor that weighs us
be our beloved's heart;
may the only arrows we strike
be towards our demons.

Worm Moon

Snowed last night, everything white, worm moon
wriggling her big belly across the backyard grass

and slick streets, lighting up a March midnight
like a friend's teeth after telling me I look better

and better each day, less devastated and dedicated
to replicating lost segments of myself. Mãe said

you were never my friend but she meant it as in
you didn't care enough to stick around and not

the way I did—as in you were my best friend,
my soulmate, the wife no one knew about

except the few who joined us five years ago in a funky
courtroom where we convinced ourselves *I do* but didn't.

Moon by moon, I wax and wane, find fullness in knowing
you were the best thing I never had, my favorite mistake,

to the left to the left, all the clichéd songs on my "Sad"
playlist I listen to as I chew on the lesson folks never want

to learn: a person is a story and stories end; lover
to wife to stranger and maybe, one day, friend.

In the Forest at Midnight

There is no right hand
tugging at the hooked fish

of my teenaged panty
no left hand

a tourniquet
on my blueing arm

no spit over
the nape of my neck

there is nothing
to forget

in this forest
at midnight

I am a gladdening choir
echoing off pines

I am thick red sap
sliding down trunks

I am glittery salt
over tree needles

I am not a child
but a loose canon

I am not a survivor
but the quiet after

I am not a body
but something unhanded

There Are Escapes and There Are True Things

like in dreams your teeth fall out and you catch them like flies in your palm in the mirror tiny fangs in their place you run to the nearest dentist and she replaces them with pearls and you smile and smile until your face breaks from all the shine and in other dreams you're a persimmon tree stretching your branches all the way up up the night sky so that it is filled with a thousand fleshy suns everyone prays to their mouths stained in rust-colored hymns

and then there's real life where your mouth is wired shut with grief lockjaw except for the coffee and pills that keep you "alive" alive moving through the day certain of nothing but the moon like a pearl and also in real life where there are no persimmon trees nothing but oak and birch and elm to chop splintered logs to warm our dry hands and cold feet on a dark winter night where nothing is kinder and truer than fire limbs over it in praise of anything and nothing

Death Is So Everywhere and So Entire

with these days, these hours strung together
like crumbs on the backs of ants, murmured fados

in the ears of Alfama, the labyrinth you never visited
or cared for; you, grandmother, got enough city in Newark,

maze of iron and river. There are so many murals here
now you'd hardly recognize it, intricate portraits of people

who'd take the number 1 bus with us, buy comforters and aprons
at ABC, boom boxes on Ferry, fresh hens at Shorty's,

bakery cookies at Pita's after. Art all along McCarter: memorials
in bright blues and heavy oranges, white dresses and electric animalia,

beautiful ghosts and graffitied gods stretching for a mile and a half
of this home when you were on earth and I wonder how many times

we walked across that highway never knowing we were getting
closer to death? How many faces it takes to remind us.

Ode to the Temporal Lobe

"You're only given a little spark of madness.
You mustn't lose it." — Robin Williams

Mighty mass of memory, how you're dulled
by the slow of traffic, dispersing of crowds,
distance between yesterday and today.
Every *whoosh, ding,* and *hum*—firework worthy
in this time of imposed still. Praise you
for the god you are to this heavy form,
hallowed receiver of word and melody; sound:
body's first language. These days, I hold fast
to caws from every blackbird in the yard, relish
every bark from my pup, crack from an egg
before the pan, hot drip of coffee in the mug,
the good and bad of screaming children,
the occasional "hello" and rare "goodbye"
like a beggar. Thank you for the myrrh
and frankincense of myth around me like smoke
when that song comes on, cause when that song
comes on: I'm not here, it's not quiet,
I'm somewhere else; it's tomorrow.

Wolf Moon

I'm the one howling at you
tonight. Howling in sorrow,

in angst, in vain and solidarity
with all other mad women

cooped up for too long
in their mortgaged houses,

in their tired bodies,
in their half-lit half the time

heads. Snapping at the
forced air, snarling every time

someone asks about dinner.
I've never been more wild

in domesticity, baring my teeth
at boredom, scratching at walls

for release. Oh, to be a cur
in the dark embrace of woods,

to run miles and miles away
from sound and screen,

to crown myself with violets
after preying, bloody mouth

a headlight in the wind.
Blame it on the patriarchy,

blame it on the pandemic,
blame it on the moon,

full and spreading herself
rabidly over us as I watch

at the window. For fuck's sake,
can't women and wolves

do that too, live fat and feral
without having to die trying?

A Valley Somewhere

Does toe around oak
doing their best to dance

unnoticed while I sneak
a photo of their pastoral

play. Outside the chaos
of the city, with its coup

of pigeons and windows
sloshed with reflections,

they are here for the same
reason: to be alone.

In the face of certain
trouble, how many times

have I wanted to yell
but knew language

a butter knife; how much
shirking is enough

to form an iron shield?
Silence has never

protected us
but whatever has in this

pleasant valley of patriarchy,
where even deer know

every man comes
armed to the party.

Aubade

Dawn peeks its head into my window,
tells Frankie it's time to yelp me awake.

I drag myself out, weary angler staring
down the hot, wet morning. My mother

says, "Foram buscar trabalho," as if work isn't
the only thing we've ever been taught

to search for. My mother says that, in
today's day and age, she wouldn't have

children, while she paints Simone's nails
Pink Sky. I don't know if I'll ever be happy

with the constant labor of love, with weaving
and mending the net, the catch and release

of grief, the plugging of barrels with carnations.
If I'll ever sit still somewhere and call it home.

Poem for When I Don't Want to be a Poet

The poet guiding the workshop meditation tells me
"Hear everything, even the absence of sound. Take a deep breath
in and turn in every direction. Take time to take in
what I am seeing, like your feet. Their contact with the earth—
is it sand, soil, rocks, or water you stand on? What is this path,
is it wide or narrow, well-traveled or hidden?"
My concentration is broken by my dog barking at the neighbor.
From the basement, I scream SHUTTHEFUCKUP. I look down
at my socks and think how dirty they are, covered in hair and dust,
crumbs and god knows. I don't want to be a poet today,
don't want to be mindful about anything except how everything
is what it is. I won't look for metaphors about how hard it is to feel
alive around so much death. No Rilke quotes or riveting image
about the cold down here, nothing but the whirring washing machine
to keep me company on this journey to my "inner self."
She's said "codicil" for the fourth time now and I decide that's enough
of words that hold no weight. I turn off the computer and cry
about my grandmother. I take off my socks, then take a bunch of selfies
in my new yellow earrings. I delete them all, wonder *Who is my inner self?*
When was the last time I swept these floors? What is life, even?

Seagull

after Amália Rodrigues's "Gaivota"

Palm to sky, torch
of blue, the readied gull
plucks every compound,
brings my breath back to you,
imperfect love so perfectly
nested in my palm (your heart
inside, an urging)
until you return
from across
the golden
ocean I worship
for holding you
so perfectly,
bold navigator,
soul conqueror,
let bird bifurcate the Atlantic
with my xailed longing
if you hear nothing
else:
this strumming blood
this burning caw

Dollar Store Mary

Protect me while I drive away
from the screaming kids and soon-to-be ex,

the dirty dishes and laundry baskets,
the work laptop and unshoveled snow,

lead me down these icy roads as I drive
to the nearest Dunkin' to get coffee and cry

in their parking lot. I need ten minutes
to spill myself, sit with the shadow grief cast

over this year, its misty hands around my neck,
its smoky legs across my ankles so that

I'm choking; I'm tripping on death.
Holy Mother dangling from the rearview,

take this body to where there is no pain
or purpose, where I can lay like a diamond

against the darkness, shining and hardened;
hide me inside the song of a sparrow,

take me into outer space, where all I hear
is the sound of my own breath, catching.

Ain't That the Way

Sun rises in the east, and ain't that the way
it sets in the west, and there are days I don't even
feel it, and ain't that the way we take shit for granted?
Take sun and air and water, like we own the shit,
ain't that the way we think we deserve the shit,
ain't that the way we ignore the shit till we destroy
the shit, like it's our God-given right, ain't that the way
shit goes, instead of praising this perfect planet
we see flower and pick it, for ain't that the way
we see bird and cage it, and ain't that the way
we see bodies and break them, for ain't that the way
we claim "Jesus is Lord, follow his way," yet commit
injustice and cry, "Love is the way," like he or it will
save us, and ain't that the way we're going to die
someday, ain't that the way if we continue this way,
ain't that the way the story of Creation ended—in exile,
ain't that the way, the only way, we seem to know

April 24

Today was supposed to be my wedding day.

Instead of walking down an aisle laced in white,
I sit alone in a gallery surrounded by portraits
of tired mothers tending to children, chided
by the only love that hasn't given them up.

I grab a blood orange, peel it slowly, bemused
to be forty and new to this fruit. Today I have
a blood orange for the first time, and it is
sweeter than I imagined. Its insides bruised,
fleshy metaphor for the hurt organ inside me.

I smuggle another into my pocket, for later.

A Wild Time

It was a wild time to be alive   Isn't that what people say
                                        when it's a year-long day
                                                of sadness, sickness, saudade?

How my hands are now   empty nests,   no egg dreams to hatch
                my feet: armoires   full of moths   No
recollection of where   they've been   just a trail of air behind   them
How with every breath we straddled
                sane and surreal;   some of us survived

How the whole year we were   tiny boats   inside bottles
tumbling around   an angry ocean,
                                        the wind: God's unsteady hand

How I will tell them the millionaire   set fire   to the dying
and the audience stood by,   some clapping,
some jeering,   and few with filled buckets   trying to put out the flames.
I will tell them

It was a wild time,
days when all I did was plant   peonies, geraniums, roses

others where I dug my grave
with a spoon

Today, or Daydream About Leaving the House

On TV, a lion-headed anchorwoman tells us
the virus morphed from freak carnation to
globe-trotting boogeyman. I am not a prefect human
but I am a perfect poet. Baraka said *poems are bullshit*
unless they are teeth so I grit mine, sand down the word
to my favorite song, decide it's time to fight mouth
to mouth, pack my notebook and a Ziploc bag
of clementines. A bedside note: *I will save us, baby.*
I will sacrifice my life for the looney, the poor, the hungry and hopeless.
You were always better with living things. Leave dying to me.

Your Blue

after Georgia O'Keeffe's Ram's Head, Blue Morning Glory, 1938

Next to me you are nothing more than a petaled palm
opening to tiny egg, breaking forth the most beautiful
flower-hand, so thin it will disintegrate if the wrong
words blow. A blue so blue—blood/beijo/oxygen.

Next to you I am nothing more than an animal's remains.
The what's-left. Brittle, pallid, remembered more for horns
than heart. Unwilling to believe the sun is no friend,
you knew my name before my father gave it to me.

We stand, mother and child. The former shattered,
you: a belled mouth open by dawn, waiting to let the world know
the secret lives of angels. Under my ready antler, no one will lift
a finger. No one will draw breath from your blue.

Vesper

They orbit around me—the loves of my life,
dervishes of calamity, mad ringmaster and
fiery acrobats, gentle giant of order and minions
of joy. I should be Happy, Full. I should be floored
with unabashed gratitude. I try to remember that
the day you plant the seed is not the day you eat the fruit
but what grows under blue light? What sings in mud?
What dances in sand but poisonous creatures?
Memories of a time when I had none of the three
sit with me while I drive, and for a moment, the thrill
of absolute freedom knocks me back. I almost cum
when I think about it. What some call greed,
I call compassion. I want all of the love
in the world from everyone and no one.
I deserve everything and nothing at the same time.

Prayer to Saint Brigid

I tear a strip of cloth
from my favorite old shirt,

brave the polar wind
and hang it on my door

so that you find us
in the whiteout,

that you mark this mantle
so it eases all ache

in the gloaming.
In this blizzarded Imbolc,

I pray, make it spring
faster, turn the snow

into scillas, the ice into ivy
spreading over houses,

so that we are encased
in breathing, bursting,

blooming things.
How long can you survive

surviving? I am ready
for the changing

of the light, for birthing
of lambs. I am ready

for life again, that messy,
moist, marvelous thing.

Matin

It isn't personal, but global. The Universe
didn't intend on making me rootstock
for sadness, the dead tiredest of the dead
tired. Monkey brain keeps me wading
in the pity pool, away from sleep while a dizzy
flock of futures rattles me from REM
with the beating of iridescence. I dream
even when I am awake, shift my foot
from one cloud to the other, until it's just
another cardboard city and I, its paper citizen.
Sing me good morrow, sparrow. Tell me one day
the egg of the sun will not crack over me
but hang like a giant pill. One day, the mother-
ship will return and not leave Earth without me.

Missing Pluto

The day Pluto was no longer considered a planet,
I decided to call God "the Force," as if a zephyr

was the only manifestation of Mother Earth
I could muster anymore. Scientists claimed

this icy sphere was too dwarfy to dominate
the neighborhood around its orbit; its moon

too microscopic compared to other moons
on other planets to be a ninth, and so excommunicated

from the church of viable worlds. I think small things
always count. Small things matter more

than we can hold in one ring, on one spin. I miss Pluto
most on days when God is a burning or a blip

missed in our collective blink. Days when I can't
conceive of anything more insignificant than myself.

Dead Things and Where to Put Them

So much to bury. So much lifelessness
carried in the pit of your belly, the bulge

of your back, the calluses of your feet.
The bird that flew into the window weeks

before your firstborn wailed into the world.
That midnight between the dark pines

and my waist and his hands. The white
currant bushes dried up by the fires.

Yellowed notebooks and fallen teeth.
The seahorses scooped out of the Atlantic,

the kit in the crow's mouth. The kittens
Avô tossed into a bag and threw

behind the shed. The onion-domed house,
the white and blue house, the chicken coop.

Your rosary, your bata, your body.
Dead things, and where to put them

if not in the ground, the damp earth
where all things return, right next to the graves

of my matriarchs whose homes are now
rubble along the roads I walked in the summers

of my youth, hands shielding child-eyes
from the unbearable light of dusk.

Tonsure

I don't know the rules
of mourning, only that
this shedding—necessary,

only that I refuse
to forget you're no longer
of this earth,

to let you go
from here once
and for all.

Every strand
to the ground—a tear
I'm unable to shed

from this dam body.
I beg baldness to
shroud me in the embers

of your pyre. To
pry me open
until I'm nothing

but glowing skin,
a pink jewel
on your tombstone.

Eulogy for the Dairy Queen on Market

Beloved, your big plastic sign
once a bat signal to all sad girls
and their grandfathers in Ironbound

who saved change after bread
and carne, eggs, leite and léxivia,
cheese and Advil, and whistle-walked

down after dinner to wait our turn
after orders of mint chocolate chip,
strawberry cream, after double fudge

finally at the window on Market
between Somme and Fillmore
before the condos and banks

urban renewal and gentrification
for *vanilla please, no sprinkles*
Avô passed me a dollar

like it was the deed to his life,
every ounce of his hard work
sliding down my rabid chin

Variation on a Theme by Rachel McKibbens

I have come to take my body from that forest, once replete of pines,
their bellies skinned, bleeding resin, orchestra of crickets, the occasional stray.

I have come to take it from his hands, dirty and callused by a dying, coughing
motorcycle; from his mouth, rank of cheap whiskey, rogue of residual wit.

I will bring my body home; bathe it first in moon water and then wine,
a libation for the ghost child looking for sheep but finding wolves.

Let this be where my body becomes mine, the bruised arms and numb cunt
and cut feet always somewhere else for years.

Let this be where my body becomes bruxa, a noose of pine around the neck
of every man who burns women at the stake of his own vulnerability.

Litany for the Surviving

after Audre Lorde

The glimmering eye of a doe greeting the morning with a yawn
reminds me of the first time I went fishing. I was eleven, it was a Wednesday
swaddled in village summer. Elisabete, Pedro, and I took our jars to the creek,
confident we'd soon be proud owners of our very own tadpoles. Before plunging
my hand in, I marveled at the sun over the water's surface: a spread of crushed
diamonds, fortress we would fist through for baby frogs. I haven't fished since,
haven't played by a body of water in years. I take long baths to escape the dry heat
of quarantine, the invisible fog of virus, the torrential national tyranny,
the impending global genocide. What if we all went fishing by a creek, or watched
deer make their way across it, praise the audacity of living? What a privilege it is
to own this imagination, this safe, white skin. How dare I think of summer,
streams, and fauna when so many have yet to know freedom of such things?
When the only thing glimmering is a black screen with breaking news.
Good God, how dare we survive ourselves, and how this?

Stray

Oh grief, you stray dog at my door
licking the rainwater off your paws
There is no room left in this house for love

No room in her heart for all four
of us, plus the pups and the fish and
oh grief, you stray dog at my door

I talk to the walls and drink
coffee at five a.m. by myself, reminded
there is no room left in this house for love

or noise, the silence booming and
barking on the longest day of the year and
oh grief, you stray dog at my door

I refuse to invite you in, refuse to let anyone
trick me again into the validity of vows
There is no room left in this house for love

I put on lipstick and a cheap ring
I am marrying myself to my sadness
Oh grief, you stray dog at my door
there is no room left in this house for love

Elegy for Maria Vicente Meireles Ribeiro

Avó waited for death like a cat at the window.
Sat in her green armchair for ten years
asking Jesus to take her back where

her father roamed the fields on horse,
where she'd sit with dogs and chickens
under a tree. "Que estou aqui a fazer,"

she'd bark after we assured her she was worth
more alive than dead. Almost a century
of cleaning, mending, cooking and mothering,

of holding books without knowing a word
of them. Death is the stuff dreams are made of
for women who fit all their joy in a thimble.

She sacrificed more than she cared to,
swallowed birds whole to keep a song inside.
No one can blame her for finally letting go,

letting her stomach fill with ocean water,
the last beating of her heart to the rooster's
morning crow. It will be all our time some time.

But oh the time, the time she loved life—
when dinner was plenty and good and we'd sit
around full and tell her stories of silly shit

we've done and she'd laugh so whole and wide
the sun would rise over her tongue,
that old yellow star blossomed against her teeth.

Ungrateful Bitch Blues

Staring out at the beautiful beyond,
trying to remember what it's like
to leave something. The benevolence

of movement. I cried last night
because I knew today would come
with all its sameness, nothingness,

its that, this, again, AGAIN.
Ungrateful bitch, I scold myself.
Count your blessings instead of sitting

crisscross applesauce and moping.
Pray your madness doesn't transfer
onto the children. They say you only

get one life, but that's not true, is it?
You live several mini-lives on
the spectrum of existence.

I've ended every one of them
by beginning. Except this one.
This one keeps on like an old red pickup.

This one rots like a tooth from the sweet
I suck out of love. This one chases
the horizon with the horse on its back.

Dearest,

after Jean Valentine

It will not unclench your jaw
or uncross your legs.
It will not loose the sparrow
back to Lisbon. This poem
will not moan Ma's blues
against your ribs. This poem
will spasm and tick and swallow
sadness, thick in the pit
of stomach. This poem
will not wash down saudade
with bitters, will not draw love
from death's vein. This poem
will not move your mouth
from the stable, will not feed you
cheese or olives or cake.
Stop trying to cry, dearest.
This poem won't offer a tissue.
This poem is grief
on its hind legs.

After Life

Are you with your father,
on his beloved mare
trotting through the serras
of São Mamede?

Are you with Avô,
and do you love him now
free of all
tricks and trespasses?

Are you a ghost
in your blue and white house
looking for the puppy
who barks your name?

I look for you
everywhere,
and everywhere
looks the same

without you.
I wait for spilled water
and red birds
to tell me

how to move on,
a mouth missing a tooth;
how to move forward
swollen with loss.

Love at the End of the World

Let's pack for everywhere tonight;
make prom of the apocalypse—
scorched dancefield where goats roam

from the dinner table, children bouquet
their grandmothers' bones, widows sing
like sparrows lost at sea—die a little death

with me on this pyre of poppy;
be the pulp people feast on, the marrow
of love staining them in Revelation.

New Year's Day

One of Pai's favorite fadistas died today.
He calls this loss "irreparável," like trees severed

from trunks, birds from their wings. Life takes
the strongest flame and blows it out. This sounds

like a fado but it's not; I'm accepting that this year
will not offer anything more or less than last.

The cold will bite, the sun shawl, rock will erode
and lives will be lost, all the same. And us,

we'll remain avatars of chaos and light. Simone
shows me her Picasso Mr. Potato Head, and I tell her

how silly it is, silly as believing that time or God
can heal a holey heart. Sometimes tears work their way

backwards, brain first. Por morrer uma andorinha
não acaba a primavera. Mais um ano passado, e já.

Sonnet for Saint Audre

Lorde, get me through this year that just started
but I fear will be too much the way last year
was too much, the way our hearts screeched like
subway trains every time we took a breath, watched
loved ones take their last. You, who taught women
are powerful and dangerous, help me make good
trouble while suffering the intense, unmitigating pain
death leaves at our door like a box of kittens.
Help me harness whatever light the shy sun delivers,
carry it with me into the cold ear of night.
Make me another kind of open, a swinger over earth;
I'll carve my name on it without making a sound.

Big Steps

I put on the cutest top I own and pinkest skirt in store
as both a *fuck you* and a *you got this, baby*. Beautiful
body coverings to convince myself one day I won't wake up
wanting to die or dreading to drape myself in anything
but the down comforter I've drowned under every night
since you left. Hell, I even moisturized my face today, balmed
my lips after brushing my teeth to train my hands to care
again for something other than the ways I picked and moved and wiped
things to make room for you in a home you never felt home in.
And tomorrow, while I put on my big leopard earrings and slide
my leather leggings up my waist, I'll tell the mirror that the only person
I ever lost and needed was myself over and over again until I believe it,
until my outside matches my inside and you can cut me in half and only
glitter and spit will spill, the aftermath of tanto tanto salvation.

Buck Moon

We are halfway through summer,
the nights growing inch by inch,
the hibiscus bloomed.

Deer cross Liberty Hall
to Ursino Park, antlers hardening
around fur, a cell phone shining

in the distance. I sit on my stoop,
think about work, parties, fast cars:
drugs of youth I no longer

long for. I'm a dream addict now,
high off gouache and pastel and poems
by Matilde Campilho.

I'm an ant chirping around
the compost of childhood, fertile earth
for my city-cum-farm girl fantasies.

My own fawns know this
glory; this forming, bony and furious,
the aftermath of survival.

I plan to die by living,
and maybe alone, but at the window
facing the orange grove and creek.

Metempsychosis

I didn't know
it was your work
at first, weaving
the silvery webs
over my door
in the dead of winter.
Every morning
I'd step outside,
greeted by a gleaming
hexagon, shield of silk
palming my face
when the sun refused
to show. These webs
went on for days, and
it wasn't until
I stood in the mirror,
looked at the thimble
tattoo that I realized
you returned
to remind me
no one ever really leaves,
that love transcends
flesh and bone and earth,
that we are forever
stitched to one another
by a thread
invisible to the ordinary.

Ooms Conservation Area

We walk, swaddled by sun and sweetgrass
trails curtained by buttercups, foxglove,
little daisies and fuchsia buds I can't name.
I am reminded of what wet earth can do.

While two talk soccer, I chew on a stalk
and think of puberty. *I have six months to live*
before my period, my oldest exclaimed recently,
with the same wariness of the oriole who flew by

on his way to nest. Bobolinks and goldfinches
cross our path, birds we are too busy to notice
in our backyards, birds my grandmother
called proof of God's imagination.

For the last mile, we coo at tiny butterflies
and dragonflies, swoon at their foamy cocoons,
how they choose the prettiest wildflower
to harness to, to breathe and grow in.

While bald eagles circle the sky, I thank my body
for carrying me through this time. I pray
Amalia is marveling too, at this moment, as she waits
on blood to show her how living beings bloom.

At the End

the lovers reunite on a bed inside the caboose of a train
headed to heaven. I'm supposed to swoon at the end
of the series, sigh and say "That's how I want to go, too,
next to my boo," but no. I want death different, alone

in my father's village, on a chair over the cobblestone
patio, blanket over my legs, one hand atop Oliver's
A Thousand Mornings, the other gripping
an orange from the grove. It will be dusk, the sky

finger-painted pink and persimmon. Before my last breath,
Avó returns down the road, JuJu panting by her side.
I smile and slack. The train behind me hoots
towards Valado. I am not in it, but still paradise bound.

Tapestry, or Now I Love Green

after Ysabel Y. González

I lay on my grass like the Vitruvian Man,
squint hard as sun films me with UV,
breathe deep enough to stir wisp off
the dandelions, stretch like a ready dancer
before debut. The Brick City in me rolls its eyes,
knows well this exercise in grounding
will last as long as my dedication to gardening.
Truth is now I love green, but I'm no good
at helping it grow. Truth is, I need nature
more than ever, to hold my body close
to earth like butter on bread, to glaze my eyes
with groves and fields so that I remember
I come from grandfolks who made so much
magic with land, who took seeds and sewed
a tapestry of orange, crimson, chameleon green.

Swing

My oldest spends hours swinging,
jackknifing the April air with her lank,

hair tossing 'round her like a peacock
fanning its feathers. While other children

chase each other, form gender-based alliances
in nonsensical games, she pummels her small

body back and forth, from one dimension
to another, eyes fixed on sky.

She springs ahead in time, to when she
can drive herself to the bookstore, buy

her own bras at Target, walk the dogs
without me. When she is not swinging,

she is climbing. Benches, slides, ladders
and walls, feet moving like beneath her—

quicksand. What is up there that wildly
excites her off the earth? What is her future

that I can't see from here, that I haven't already
dreamt in a thousand dreams? I don't know

how to make ground safe enough for rooting.
How to tether a child who refuses to be an island.

Desgraçada

A persimmon where a heart should be.
But this doesn't mean I can't live.
Avó taught me the greatest of truths:
we are just books of bone, muscled myths.
Once these bodies break down to dust,
we are sounds and letters and laughter
in someone's mouth, and someone else's.
We are stories beloveds tell on the porch,
by the river, walking a dog. *But you're at*
the beginning, baby! And until you're only
words to be remembered by, be
fruit tree, be train, be bird and storm.

To the Baby Rabbits in My Backyard

You will not remember this overcast
sky where rain breaks through the sun
every so often, turning the hard earth
to sloppy mud, nor this delicate moment,
when I lifted a patch of damp grass to reveal
five of you, soft black and squirming
with the same queries for the Universe
we hold. Before I marveled at the sight
of your buttoned eyes and tiny ears, bodies
sleek with new fur and soil, before I looked up
at the heavens to check for crows, before
I begged this manicured yard to keep you warm,
I sighed so goddamn hard my heart combusted.
I've been holding myself in for weeks now
from fear that nothing will be the same again
because nothing will be the same again.
There are so many things we aren't meant to survive,
but I swallow the vinegar with the honey
and lower the clump back down, pat the earth
you lie under in wait, and sit by my window
for the rest of the day, waiting on your mother.

Acknowledgments

Sincere gratitude for the following publications, where some of the work in this collection first appeared:

Digging Press: "Folklore"

Ghost Peach Press: "Cathexis" and "Pandemic"

Limp Wrist: "Dearest,"; "Ode to the Deer on the Side of the Road as America"; "Death is So Everywhere and So Entire"

The Newarker: "Newark Penn Station"

The Night Heron Barks: "Dead Things and Were to Put Them" and "Stray"

Pensive: A Global Journal of Spirituality & The Arts: "Exulansis"

Taint Taint Taint Magazine: "Prayer to Saint Brigid"

Obrigada

Highest praise to my Higher Power, through which I can do all things. To Amalia and Simone, my sun and my moon, my best friends on this journey: my love for you is infinite and out of this world. To Pai, Mae, and Suzy: your love and support are tantamount to my success, and I am eternally grateful and amo-vos muito. To Sam, my sunflower, for seeing me in every moment. Chee amo. To Emiley, Lynne, Elisabete, and Valentina: your sisterhood sustains me and I love you deeply. To my peoples: Ysabel, Tamara, Kat, Grisel, Claudia, Dimitri, Roberto, Vincent, Patrick, Danny, Diane, Cris, Chenoa, Goncalo, Arielle, Maria, Rey, Cindy, Laura, James, Carla Sofia, Sharon, Rosibel, Tashiya, Ashley, Mary, Uzma, Walter, Jessica, Vicel, Christopher, Danielle, Sonia, Kween, Attorious, Danielle, Lily, Luisa, my Rutgers folks, my Disquiet Crew; and if I forgot your name on this list, you know I love you, blame my (air) head and not my (full) heart. To Dr. Gray and my COE family: thank you for encouraging my professional- and personal- growth. To my blurbers and fellow writers Casey, Angelique, and Claudia: your kindness is everything and so is your work! To Cavankerry—Joan, Gabriel, Dimitri, Dana, Tamara, Baron, Mike, and Toma—y'all are a gift to poetry! To my poetry mothers, Audre Lorde, Rachel McKibbens, Mary Oliver: my art would not exist without your masterpieces. To you, Reader: may this book bring you closer to the changing of the light, the birthing of lambs.

CavanKerry's Mission Page

A not-for-profit literary press serving art and community, CavanKerry is committed to expanding the reach of poetry and other fine literature to a general readership by publishing works that explore the emotional and psychological landscapes of everyday life, and to bringing that art to the underserved where they live, work, and receive services.

Other Books in the Florenz Eisman Memorial Series

The Curve of Things, Kathy Kremins
Tanto Tanto, Marina Carreira
Wonderama, Catherine Doty
WORKS, Danny Shot
Abloom & Awry, Tina Kelley

This book was printed on paper from responsible sources.

Dead Things and Where to Put Them is typeset in Miller Text, a serif created in 1997 by US-based type foundry, the Font Bureau. Its design is inspired by the Scotch Roman typefaces of the 1800s made by companies such as Miller & Richard, to which it owes its name.